CONTENTS

KU-390-309

A sport of skill

Football is a sport full of excitement, energy and drama where matches can be won and lost in a split-second. Football players need to develop the skills necessary to take part. These skills include the ability to control the ball, as well as how to spot gaps and weaknesses in the opposition team.

Pitch and players

A football pitch measures up to 120 metres long and 70 metres wide. With 22 players on two sides competing for the ball, even this large area can still feel crowded. Players try to space themselves out by playing in various positions, such as defence, midfield and attack. Players in different positions need different skills – defenders need to be strong tacklers, while attackers need to be good at shooting.

ON THE BALL

FIFA World
Player of the Year
award winners:
2010:
Men's – Lionel Messi
Women's – Marta
2009:
Men's – Lionel Messi
Women's – Marta

A goalkeeper practises saving shots during training. Goalkeepers need different skills from other players on the pitch. They need to be agile in order to make diving saves and they need to be good at catching the ball.

FOOTBALL FOCUS

PLAYERS AND SKILLS

14 FEB

15

Clive Gifford

BROMLEY LIBRARIES

3 0128 70091 7936

First published in 2009 by Wayland

This paperback edition updated and
published in 2011 by Wayland

Copyright © Wayland 2009

Wayland
Hachette Children's Books
338 Euston Road
London NW1 3BH

Wayland Australia
Level 17/207 Kent Street
Sydney, NSW 2000

All rights reserved.

Editor: Julia Adams
Produced by Tall Tree Ltd
Editor, Tall Tree: Jon Richards
Designer: Ben Ruocco

British Library Cataloguing in Publication Data

Gifford, Clive.
  Players and skills. -- (Football focus)
  1. Soccer--Juvenile literature. 2. Soccer players--
  Juvenile literature.
  I. Title II. Series
  796.3'342-dc22

ISBN: 9780750266949

Printed in China

Wayland is a division of Hachette Children's Books,
an Hachette UK company.

www.hachette.co.uk

Acknowledgements

The author and publisher would like to thank the
following people for their help and participation in this
book: Whiteknights FC, Eric Burrow, Steve Rendell and
Paul Scholey

Picture credits

All photographs taken by Michael Wicks, except;
t - top, l - left, r - right, b - bottom, c - centre
cover t - Dreamstime.com, tr - Dreamstime.com/Moori,
bl - Dreamstime.com/Putnik70, tl - Dreamstime.
com/Miflippo, c - Dreamstime.com/Ginosphotos, 1
Dreamstime.com/Lario Tus, 2 Dreamstime.com/Fabrizio
Mariani, 4 Dreamstime.com/Santamaradona, 5
Dreamstime.com/Diademimages, 6 Dreamstime.com/Jose
Gil, 7 Mitchell Layton/NewSport/Corbis, 8 Dreamstime.
com/Diademimages, 15 Duomo/Corbis, 17 Dreamstime.
com/Diademimages, 18 Dreamstime.com/Diademimages,
20 Dreamstime.com/Fabrizio Mariani, 25 Dreamstime.
com/Lario Tus, 28 Dreamstime.com/Dong Hj, 30
Dreamstime.com/Diademimages, 32 Dreamstime.com/
Diademimages

The website addresses (URLs) included in this book were
valid at the time of going to press. However, because
of the nature of the Internet, it is possible that some
addresses may have changed, or sites may have changed
or closed down since publication. While the author and
publisher regret any inconvenience this may cause to
readers, no responsibility for any such changes can be
accepted by either the author or the publisher.

Disclaimer

In preparation of this book, all due care has been
exercised with regard to the advice, activities and
techniques depicted. The publishers regret that they can
accept no liability for any loss or injury sustained. When
learning a new sport it is important to get expert tuition
and to follow a manufacturer's instructions.

Starting out

Many star footballers began playing fun games with their friends in the streets and parks and on the beaches near their homes. Small-sided games, such as five-a-side, help to build basic skills. These skills are then worked on with coaches in training at schools and clubs. As players progress and play for better and better teams, they never stop practising their core skills, even if they get to play for their countries. These skills include being able to pass quickly and accurately with both feet, control the ball as they twist and turn, shoot strongly and head the ball well.

❝ *I think the best way to improve your skills is to play football on a smaller pitch. I didn't play 11-a-side football until I was 13. On a small pitch you need to have good control and move the ball around quickly. There isn't much space so you need to be skilful.*

Brazilian footballing star
Juninho **❞**

French footballer Franck Ribéry (in blue) runs at two Dutch defenders during a 2006 international match. Ribéry has great skills and balance and is known for running at opponents with the ball under close control.

Fit and fast

Football is an athletic, high-intensity sport, so players need to be very fit to perform at their best throughout a match. Even the most expert players have to practise their skills and improve their fitness.

In training

Professional footballers carry out different types of training to develop their physical fitness, strength and skills. Players work on their strength and stamina in the gym and in outdoor sessions. Pace is very important in football, which is why training will include sprinting practice. Players also perform drills and play small games while training, in order to develop skills such as shooting, tackling and passing. All of these drills are carried out under the watchful eye of the team's coach.

> *Do you have the heart to push yourself? If you don't, find a way to get it because talent will only get you so far.*
>
> US striker
> **Tiffeny Milbrett**

Chelsea players warm up before a training session by lightly jogging around the pitch. Warming up is a vital part of training as it prepares a player's muscles, lungs and heart for the hard exercise ahead.

ON THE BALL

At the 2002 World Cup, Spain could not play their first-choice goalkeeper, Santiago Cañizares, as he injured his foot by dropping a bottle on it.

Injuries and prevention

Football injuries are a concern for players and teams – an injured player will not be able to play, possibly for a long time. Most injuries are caused to the ankle and knee joints or the leg muscles. They can vary from a dead leg (a leg feeling numb because of a collision) to broken bones or torn ligaments. Such serious injuries can see a player unable to play for many months. Warming up and performing a lot of stretches before a match or heavy training session can prevent a lot of muscle injuries.

American player Brandi Chastain had to walk with crutches after breaking a bone in her right foot during a Women's World Cup match.

Playing positions

A football team is divided into the goalkeeper and the 10 outfield players, who line up in a pattern called a formation. This pattern consists of rows of defenders, midfielders and attackers.

Defenders

Defenders are expected to stop opposition attacks, so they need to be good at heading, marking (see page 20) and clearances (kicking or heading the ball away from their own goal). They should also be very skilled at anticipating an opponent's movement and making committed, decisive challenges without fouling the attacking opposition player.

ON THE BALL

Defenders can help their forwards by joining an attack. Dutch defender Ronald Koeman scored a staggering 207 goals during his career, including 14 for his national team.

goalkeeper

central defenders

full back

midfielders

attackers

Team formations are described by the numbers of defenders, midfielders and attackers, so the formation shown here is known as 4-4-2 (four defenders, four midfielders and two attackers).

Midfielders and attackers

Midfielders need to work on their fitness, as they help out both in defence and attack, covering more ground than any other players. They will receive a lot of passes as the ball moves back and forwards between defence and attack, so they should be good at controlling the ball. Attackers need to be very good at scoring goals. They should be able to shoot and head the ball accurately and they should also be able to spot good positions on the pitch where they will be in space to receive a pass and launch an attack.

Manchester United and England attacker Wayne Rooney (in white) gets past the tackle of a United States defender. Rooney has developed the skills needed to be a good attacker, so he is able to shoot from long distances and get into spaces from where he can score.

Passing

Quick passing can see a team keep the ball, move it past opponents and get into a position to score. Passing is the most common skill used in a game. The 2010 World Cup Final saw Spain and the Netherlands make a total of 973 passes with one player, Spain's Xavi, making 97 by himself.

> " Football is a simple game based on the giving and taking of passes, of controlling the ball and of making yourself available to receive a pass.
>
> legendary Liverpool football manager **Bill Shankly** "

Longer passing and weight

Sometimes during a match you might want to send a pass across the entire width of the pitch. The high, lofted pass is best for this, using the top of the foot (where the boot laces are) to lift the ball off the ground and send it over a long distance. You should get your body over the ball and swing your leg through the ball so that your boot laces strike the middle of it. The amount of force put into a pass is called its weight. Getting the weight of a pass right is very important, especially when passing the ball ahead of another player for them to run onto. Too much weight can see the ball go out of play. Too little, and an opposing player could intercept the pass.

Lofted pass

To make a lofted pass, this player has hit the ball with the top of her boot. She has also leant back, which will put more height onto her pass.

Sidefoot pass

1 These two players are taking part in a simple drill to practise their sidefoot passes. Player 1 is passing to player 2. He turns his kicking foot sideways and makes contact with the ball using the side of his foot.

2 After player 1 has made contact with the ball, he follows through, pushing his foot, which is still turned sideways, towards player 2 to make sure that the pass is accurate. Player 2 will make a sidefoot pass back.

Short passes

The most common pass in football is the sidefoot pass. This sees the ball rolled across the pitch using the inside of the boot. Because the whole side of the foot comes into contact with the ball, it is the most accurate pass, but is best used over shorter distances. Flick passes can change the ball's direction. Flicks are usually made with the outside of the boot. They have very little power and are used only over short distances.

Player power

It is vital that you work hard at passing with both feet. During a match you may not have the time or space to use your favoured foot. Being able to pass with both feet allows you to move the ball all over the pitch and makes it harder for opponents to challenge you.

Flick pass

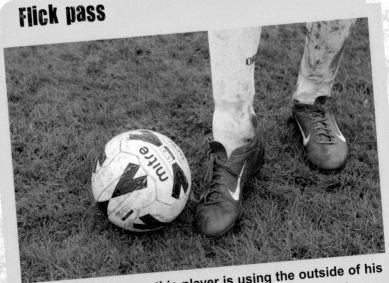

To make a flick pass, this player is using the outside of his boot. The kicking foot is swivelled quickly at the ankle. This nudges, or flicks, the ball to one side.

Ball control

The receiver is the player to whom a pass is made. In some situations, a receiver's first touch of the ball is an immediate pass or header to a team-mate. Usually, though, the receiving player first aims to control the ball in order to make a pass, shoot or run.

Player power

In attack, sometimes you can pretend that you are going to control the ball, but let the ball roll past you and follow it with a quick change of direction instead. This can trick a defender into going the wrong way.

Cushioning

You can use any part of your body to control the ball, with the exception of your hands and arms. If you do use your hands or arms, the referee will signal handball and the opposition will be awarded a free-kick. However, if you handle the ball in your own penalty area and your action was considered deliberate, the opposition will be awarded a penalty and you could receive a yellow card or even a red card. To control the ball and slow it down, players use a skill called cushioning. The part of the body making contact with the ball is moved away from the ball as it arrives. This will slow the ball's impact and leave it under control at your feet. Cushioning using the side of the foot, the top of the thigh and the chest are the most common.

This player is receiving a pass and bringing it under control using his foot. As the ball arrives, he moves his right foot back down with the ball to slow the ball's fall so that it drops at his feet and under control.

" *Football is a team game and it's the whole team that should take credit, not just individual players. Every member of the squad plays their part and as a team we win together or we lose together.*

England striker
Wayne Rooney
"

Thigh control

This player is controlling a pass using his thigh. The player raises his thigh to meet the ball and then pulls it down with the ball to slow the ball's fall.

Chest control

1 If the pass is quite high, you might have to use your chest to control the ball. As the pass arrives, this player sticks out his chest to receive the ball.

2 Just as the ball arrives, the player pulls back his chest to cushion the ball. At the same time, he brings his shoulders forwards to stop the ball bouncing off to one side.

Firm control

In some situations, players try not to stop the ball dead, but change its direction instead. This is known as firm control. The part of the body that connects with the ball is kept firm and thrust forwards as the ball arrives. By using firm control, a player can, for example, make a rapid pass over a short distance with their chest, twisting the upper body to steer the ball in the right direction.

13

Shielding, running and turning

Once a player has received and controlled the ball, they need to make their next move. In many situations, the player may shield the ball, run or turn with the ball.

Shielding

Sometimes, a player will receive a pass and immediately find themselves under pressure from an opponent. They can either pass the ball before the opponent can challenge them or protect the ball by shielding it. This is where the player puts their body between the opponent and the ball while keeping the ball under control. Keeping control of the ball is vital. If the player is not close to the ball and they use their body in this way, the referee will signal obstruction and award a free-kick to the opposition.

ON THE BALL

Top players can run more than 10 kilometres during a 90-minute match. At Euro 2008, Dutch midfielder Rafael van der Vaart ran 14.73 kilometres during a single game.

Shielding the ball

1 This attacker (in blue) is in possession of the ball and the defender (in yellow) stands close by to try to slow him down.

2 The attacker makes sure that he keeps himself between the defender and the ball, shielding it with his body.

3 While shielding the ball, the attacker can make a short pass to a team-mate on one side or the other.

Player power

A drag back turn lets you trick defenders. Pretend you are going to play the ball in one direction, but stop the ball's movement with the sole of your boot. Then drag the ball back and pivot on your standing foot. Now head off in a different direction.

Running and turning

A player running with the ball tries to keep their body in between the ball and any arriving opponent. When free of opposition players, they may push the ball in front, ready to change direction or to protect the ball. If they have a lot of space in front of them and no opponents within close range, a player may push the ball farther ahead so that they can sprint harder. They try to keep their head up, watching where team-mates and opponents are in order to work out their next move. There are several ways that a player with the ball can turn to change direction. They can pivot round with one foot on the ball, or they can overrun the ball, cut back and change direction quickly.

Abby Wambach of Washington Freedom shows good technique while running with the ball. Her head is up and she is looking around for any of her team-mates to pass to and for any opposition players who may try to challenge her.

Crossing and heading

A cross is a long, high pass from near the sidelines into the penalty area. Crosses are very useful for getting the ball behind the defenders and close to goal, where attackers are more likely to score.

ON THE BALL

In the first 30 games of the 2010/11 English Premier League season, Matthew Jarvis of Wolverhampton Wanderers made the most crosses of any player – 295 or nearly 10 per game.

Crossing options

Crosses are aimed a little above head height, so that a team-mate can run in and head the ball. The player crossing the ball needs to be aware of team-mates' positions before making a cross. Sometimes, it may not be possible to cross the ball straight away. There may be a defender blocking the ball's path or no team-mates in the penalty area to aim for. In these situations, a player may try to sprint past a defender down the sideline before making a cross.

Crossing into the penalty area

1 Here, a player is making a cross from near the side of the pitch, using his left foot to make a lofted pass (see page 10). By leaning back, he gets plenty of height onto his cross.

2 The high ball puts taller attackers at an advantage. The tall attacker (in blue) can easily jump higher than shorter defenders and head the ball towards goal.

Heading the ball

During a match, the ball will spend a lot of time in the air, so heading is a vital skill in attack and defence. Players aim to meet the middle of the ball with their forehead and try to watch the ball right up to the moment of impact. A defensive header is aimed high and with as much power as possible to clear the ball. An attacking header towards goal sees the player try to get their head above the ball so that they can direct it down and away from the goalkeeper.

" *The art of heading for goal is to use your whole body to get as much power into your header as you can. Don't just let the ball bounce off your head. Use your whole body by bending your knees, arching your back and tensing your neck muscles, and then thrust forward on contact.* "

Manchester United midfielder
Gary Neville

Even players who are experts at controlling the ball with their feet must learn to head the ball with confidence and power. Portugal and Real Madrid winger Cristiano Ronaldo (in red) is well known for his dribbling skills, but he is also a superb header of the ball.

Goalkeeping

Goalkeepers need a lot of concentration, bravery and lightning reactions. Top keepers alert their team-mates to danger. They also take control when defending corners and free-kicks, telling defenders where to go.

Positioning and handling

While spectacular diving saves are the most memorable part of goalkeepers' play, most of their work involves being in the right position when the opposition attacks and making sure that they catch any crosses cleanly. Keepers aim to get their bodies in line with the direction of the ball. This means that their bodies form a second barrier if the ball bounces out of their hands. Once the ball is in their hands, goalkeepers can roll the ball out underarm, throw it out overarm or kick it from their hands.

ON THE BALL

A clean sheet is when a keeper does not let in a goal during a game. In April 2010, Petr Cech kept his 100th clean sheet for Chelsea in just 180 matches.

Miguel Calero of Mexican side Pachuca makes a dramatic save against United States side DC United. Goalkeepers need to be athletic and supple to pull off such difficult saves.

Catches, punches and deflections

Keepers practise catching the ball at different heights and angles. These catches range from stretching up to grab a high ball to dropping on one knee to gather in a ball rolling across the pitch. At all times during a game, a keeper focuses on the play, watching the ball and always prepared for an attack. Sometimes, a keeper decides they cannot catch the ball securely. In these cases, they make a punch to clear the ball or deflect it over the crossbar or around the post.

" I watch the games on television in the evening. I'll study, for example, a cross from the second half, or a corner in the first half, and look at how I can improve my anticipation or positioning by even the smallest fraction.

Manchester United keeper
Edwin van der Sar "

Goalkeeping practice

Catching high balls (above) requires plenty of concentration. The keeper should watch the ball all the way into his hands, to stop it from slipping out.

When fielding a low ball (above), the keeper drops to one knee and gets his body behind the ball to create a second barrier behind his hands. He watches the ball right into his hands.

Kicking is an important part of keeping (left), as a keeper may have to clear the ball quickly when challenged by the opposition.

Tackling and defending

Players have to defend when they lose possession of the ball. They must cut down the space their opponents have to attack, stop goals being scored and try to recover the ball.

Marking and blocking

Defenders stick close to individual opponents and follow their movements to prevent them getting into space to receive a pass. This is called marking. When an opponent does have the ball, the aim is to stop them turning to face goal. Defenders may sometimes jump in the way to block a shot or an attacking pass.

ON THE BALL

Nigel Reo-Coker of English club Aston Villa made 178 successful tackles during 2007-08 - more than any other player in the English Premier League that season.

Defenders have to work together as a unit to stop attacks. Here, the defenders of Siena (in black and white) are closing down Clarence Seedorf from AC Milan (in red) during an Italian Serie A game.

Tackling

When a player challenges for the ball, they need to be strong and decisive. The front block is the most common form of tackle (see right). Another is the side tackle (see below). When an opponent is running with the ball, it may be possible to kick the ball out of their control using a side tackle. Defenders try to stay on their feet. The sliding tackle sees defenders slide along the ground, and it is used only as a last resort. With all tackles, care has to be taken to connect with the ball and not the attacking player, otherwise the defender will give away a foul and the opposition will be awarded a free-kick.

Front block

1 The defender (in yellow) places his left foot firmly, bending the knee slightly to get his weight over the ball.

2 He then strikes the ball with his right foot, knocking it away, while making sure not to touch the attacker.

Side tackle

1 The defender (in yellow) picks his moment to tackle carefully so as not to give away a foul.

2 He moves in and makes a firm challenge for the ball using the side of his foot.

3 Taking care not to foul the attacker, he knocks the ball clear.

The defender (in yellow) has chosen to use a sliding tackle. Sliding tackles are very risky and take a lot of skill, so they should be performed only as a last resort. The defender slides in on his left leg, extending his right leg to clear the ball out of the control of his opponent.

Attacking skills

Attackers with the ball have a lot of responsibility. They do not want to give the ball away easily, but they also want to continue the attack, taking the ball into more dangerous positions to try to score.

ON THE BALL

Javier Hernandez of Mexico is one of the world's fastest footballers. During one match at the 2010 World Cup, he was measured sprinting at 32.15km/h.

Attacking techniques

While passing can create chances to score, there are other techniques that attackers can use as well. A player can fake a pass to trick a defender into moving the wrong way, before driving forwards with the ball and taking a shot. Another way of beating an opponent is called the push-and-go. This works only if there is a lot of space behind an opponent. The attacker pushes the ball past the defender and into the open space. They then sprint hard to collect the ball. A variation of this move, known as a nutmeg, involves passing the ball between the defender's legs.

Balance and control are very important when attacking with the ball. Here players are practising their dribbling skills by moving the ball in and out through a line of poles.

Dribbling and tricks

Dribbling is moving while keeping the ball under close control with a series of nudges and taps. It is very risky and should be performed only in areas close to the other team's goal. Players like Cristiano Ronaldo and Nani are highly skilled at adding swerves, stepovers and changes of speed and direction to their dribbling. The aim is to confuse or unbalance a defender, making it easier to dribble and sprint past them.

> **It is important when dribbling to use both feet. Make sure you use the outside, inside and soles of your feet. Make sure you stay on your toes, bend your knees and keep your head up.**
>
> England winger
> **Rachel Yankey**

Stepovers

1 As the ball is rolling forwards, the attacker moves his left foot over the ball, taking care not to touch it.

2 When the left foot comes down, the attacker's right foot moves around behind the ball.

3 The attacker places his left foot and can now change direction, moving the ball away quickly to his right.

4 Alternatively, he can step over the ball again, this time with his right foot, to try to confuse and unbalance a nearby defender and make him lunge for the ball.

Movement and vision

Attacking players should always try to make attacking runs, from where they can create opportunities to score. They should also get into positions away from defenders where they can receive a pass and launch an attack.

Getting free

Any attacking run must be well timed and performed sharply to shake off a defender standing close by. Attackers use changes of direction and vary their running speed to get free of a defender. Another technique is to fake intentions. This is when an attacker leans one way and appears to be heading in that direction, but sprints away in a different direction instead.

ON THE BALL

In 2008, David Beckham, playing for United States team LA Galaxy, showed great technique and awareness to score with a shot 60 metres from the goal.

Chipping over the defence

1 The attackers (in blue) are aiming to get behind the defender (in yellow). Attacker 1 chooses to play a short lofted kick, called a chip, over the top of the defender.

2 Attacker 1 stabs down with his foot on the bottom half of the ball to chip it over the defender's head. Attacker 2 times his run to meet the pass. The ball and the attacker are now behind the defender and the attack can be continued.

Width and vision

Using the sides, or flanks, of the pitch is a great way to get the ball behind a defence. Attackers can make overlapping runs down the flanks with the ball passed ahead of them to run onto. Players can work together to pass and move rapidly, using sharp running and quick, precise touches to move the ball around the pitch and past defenders. In order to carry these moves out successfully, however, players must have vision. This is an awareness of what is going on around them and the ability to spot a possible attacking pass or space to move into.

> " It's sometimes appropriate to pass to a team-mate and I'll always do that. I guess a good striker will take the shot 80 per cent of the time. But forwards have to know the best position and get there in the most efficient way. It's football intelligence. "
>
> French attacker
> **Fredi Kanouté**

Luka Modric of Croatia (in red and white) makes an attacking run against a Moldovan defender. Modric is well known for making such attacking runs and for his control of the ball with both feet. He is also very good at getting into attacking positions when he does not have the ball.

Shooting and scoring

It is vital that all footballers practise shooting and scoring goals accurately. All players, including defenders and midfielders, may get a chance to shoot during a match.

ON THE BALL

Gerd Müller scored 365 goals in just 427 league matches for German side Bayern Munich. He also scored 68 goals in just 62 games for West Germany.

Player power

All players, including world-class strikers, miss easy chances to score. Put a bad miss out of your mind and focus on taking the next chance you get to score.

Shooting skills

Shooting relies on quick reactions to get a shot off before a defender can tackle or block. It also relies on good placement of the shot, such as aiming the ball away from the goalkeeper and towards the empty corners of the goal. Shooting too high is a common problem. This can often be corrected by getting the body over the ball and remembering not to lean back as the shot is made.

The easiest way to place a shot is using the side of the foot. However, this will not put a lot of power into the shot, so it should be used only at close range, as shown by this attacker (in blue).

Volleys and other shots

A ball struck while in mid-air is known as a volley. A well-struck volley can result in an unstoppable shot. A half-volley is where the ball is struck just as it bounces, but the resulting shot can be just as powerful as a volley. Shots are not always powerful drives and volleys. Chip shots are when players dig their kicking feet sharply into the bottom of the ball to send it up and over a goalkeeper. Other goals are scored when attackers, with their back to goal, simply backheel the ball into the net.

Hitting a front-on volley

1 As the ball arrives, the attacker keeps his eye on it and pulls back his shooting leg.

2 He keeps his kicking foot pointing down and he keeps his head over the ball to stop his shot flying into the air.

3 He aims to strike the ball with his boot laces and, after kicking the ball, his leg follows through.

Here, an attacker (in blue) has realised that he cannot reach a cross with his foot. As a result, he has thrown himself to perform a diving header and put the ball past the keeper.

Set-piece skills

Set-pieces are ways of restarting a match after a stoppage or because the ball has run off the pitch. Teams spend lots of time practising set-pieces, because they often result in a goal.

Free-kicks

A free-kick is awarded to a team when opposition players have broken one of the game's laws. The team awarded the free-kick can either shoot or pass the ball, depending on where the free-kick has been awarded. Many free-kicks see the ball launched high into the other team's penalty area. If the free-kick is close to goal, the attacking players may try to shoot directly at the goal, bending or swerving the ball so that it curves around the edge of a defensive wall and towards goal.

ON THE BALL

Some goalkeepers have becomes famous free kick and penalty takers. In March 2011, goalkeeper, Rogerio Ceni scored his 100th goal for Brazilian team, Santos.

A Chinese attacker (in red) has taken a free-kick against Vietnam (in white). He has bent the ball over and around the wall of defenders shielding the goal.

28

Corners

A corner is awarded when the ball goes out of play across the goal line and a defender was the last player to touch the ball. Corners can be hit short to a nearby team-mate or crossed long into the penalty area. A corner taker normally uses the lofted pass (see page 10) and tries to get enough height on the ball for a team-mate to make a header. Team-mates aim to time their runs so that they can meet the ball with a header at the goal.

> " *Take a good look at your players and decide who can deliver the right ball. Decide what type of delivery you want, i.e. inswinger, outswinger or just chipped to the near post, and choose who can deliver the ball.* "
>
> West Ham United academy coach **Tony Carr** on taking corners

Taking corners

1 As the player taking the corner moves in to cross the ball into the penalty area, his team-mates try to get free of the defenders who are marking them.

2 The corner taker has the option to curve the ball in towards the goal (an inswinging corner) or away from the goal (an outswinging corner).

What it takes to be...

A top player

Marta Vieira da Silva

Marta was discovered while playing football at the age of 14. She gained experience and improved her skills in youth and first teams of three Brazilian women's clubs. At only 1.54 metres tall, Marta had to work hard to succeed against bigger, stronger opponents. She sometimes played in midfield but is now renowned as a goal-scoring striker with pace, great dribbling skills and a powerful shot.

Career path

- ⚽ 2001 Wins the Under 19 Brazil Championship with Vasco da Gama team.

- ⚽ 2004 Moves to leading Swedish women's team, Umeå IK.

- ⚽ 2006 Voted by FIFA as the world's best female footballer at the age of 20.

- ⚽ 2008 Wins her third World Footballer of the Year title.

- ⚽ 2009 Moves to United States club Los Angeles Sol to play in the first season of Women's Professional Soccer.

During the 2007 Women's World Cup, Marta finished as the competition's top scorer and was voted its best player.

Glossary

chip lifting the ball over an opposition player by stabbing downwards on the underside of the ball. Chips are used for short passes or for shots on goal.

coach someone who works with the players, deciding who should play and what tactics to use. A coach does not get involved in any business aspects of the football club.

corner awarded to an attacking team when the ball crosses the goal line and a defender was the last player to touch the ball. A corner is taken from inside a small quadrant in the corner of the pitch on the side where the ball went out of play.

dribbling running with the ball under control, nudging it forwards using light touches so that it does not get too far ahead and out of control.

free-kick a way of restarting a game. Referees award free-kicks to a team when the opposition commits a foul or breaks one of the laws of the game.

marking to stand close to opposition players and follow their movements closely, making sure that they do not get into enough space to receive a pass.

nutmeg kicking the ball between the legs of an opposition player and collecting the ball on the other side.

set-pieces ways of restarting a game after the ball has left play or a foul has been committed. Set-pieces include free-kicks, corners and throw-ins.

striker a team's best goal scorer and the player who usually plays nearest the opposition goal.

Books

Sporting Skills: Football by Clive Gifford (Wayland, 2008)
Skills of the Game: Football by Jim Kelman (Wayland, 2006)
Training to Succeed: Football by Edward Way (Franklin Watts, 2009)
Inside Sport: Football by Clive Gifford (Wayland, 2007)

Websites

www.talkfootball.co.uk
Website with photos and videos of skills.
http://news.bbc.co.uk/sport1/hi/football/skills/default.stm

Watch videos and read tips from star players.
www.thefa.com
Information on football in your area and advice on developing skills and fitness.

Index